The Pond

Written by Hannah Reed

sundance

A Haights Cross Communications Company

This is a pond.
Lots of things
live in the pond.

Plants live
in the pond.

This tadpole lives
in the pond.

It eats plants
that live
in the pond.

This duck lives
in the pond.

It eats plants
that live
in the pond.

This snail lives
in the pond.

It eats plants
that live
in the pond.

This frog lives
in the pond.

It eats snails
that live
in the pond.

This fish lives
in the pond.

It eats tadpoles
that live
in the pond.

Pond Life

is food for   is food for

is food for